COLOR AND LEARN THE BEAUTIFUL NAMES OF ALLAH

A Coloring Book for Children

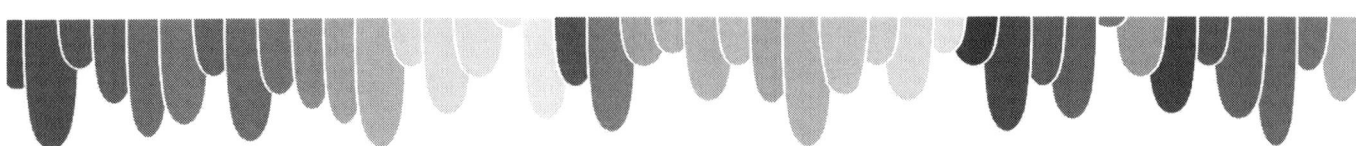

The Explanation to the Beautiful and Perfect Names of Allah by Shaykh Sa'di, rahimahullah,
with additional names added by Shaykh Saalih al-Uthaymeen, rahimahullah.

Every name We have used has been backed up with dalil from the Qur'aan and/or authentic ahadith

Let children memorise and understand the meaning and implication of each Beautiful Name of Allah

Please note : this is not Al Asma Ul Husna (99 Names of Allah Ta'ala)

Published By: The Way of Islam, 6 Cave Street, Preston, Lancashire, PR1 4SP

ALLAH

THE ONE GOD, THE ONLY ONE DESERVING OF WORSHIP

اللَّهُ لَا إِلَهَ إِلَّا هُوَ

Allah! La ilaaha illa Huwa (none has the right to be worshipped but He) (2:255)

ADH-DHAAHIR
THE UPPERMOST

هُوَ الأَوَّلُ وَالآخِرُ وَالظَّاهِرُ وَالْبَاطِنُ ۖ وَهُوَ بِكُلِّ شَيْءٍ عَلِيمٌ

He is the First (nothing is before Him) and the Last (nothing is after Him), the Uppermost (nothing is above Him) and the Innermost (nothing is nearer than Him). And He is the All-Knowing (57:3)

AL-AAKHIR
THE LAST

الآخِر

هُوَ الْأَوَّلُ وَالْآخِرُ وَالظَّاهِرُ وَالْبَاطِنُ ۖ وَهُوَ بِكُلِّ شَيْءٍ عَلِيمٌ

He is the First (nothing is before Him) and the Last (nothing is after Him), the Uppermost
(nothing is above Him) and the Innermost (nothing is nearer than Him). And He is the All-Knowing (57:3)

AL-'AALIM

THE ALL-KNOWER (OF THE SEEN AND THE UNSEEN)

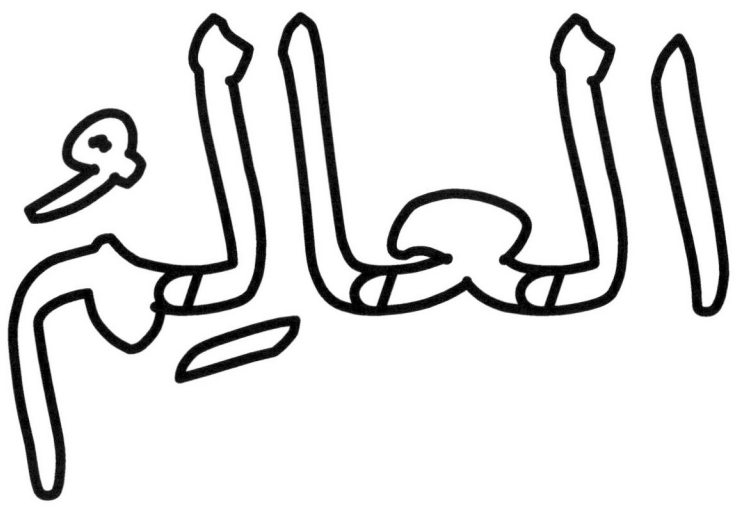

عَالِمُ الْغَيْبِ وَالشَّهَادَةِ

All-Knower of the unseen and the seen ... (6:73)

AL-'ADHEEM

THE MAGNIFICENT

فَسَبِّحْ بِاسْمِ رَبِّكَ الْعَظِيمِ

Then glorify with praises the Name of your Lord, the Magnificent. (56:74)

AL-'AFUWW

THE ONE WHO CONTINUES TO FORGIVE

إِن تُبْدُوا خَيْرًا أَوْ تُخْفُوهُ أَوْ تَعْفُوا عَن سُوءٍ فَإِنَّ اللَّهَ كَانَ عَفُوًّا قَدِيرًا

Whether you disclose a good deed, or conceal it, or forgive an evil.

Verily, Allah is One Who continues to forgive, All-Powerful (4:149)

AL-AHAD
THE UNIQUE

وَلَمْ يَكُن لَّهُ كُفُوًا أَحَدٌ

And there is none co-equal or comparable unto Him. (112:4)

AL-AKRAM

THE MOST GENEROUS

اقْرَأْ وَرَبُّكَ الْأَكْرَمُ الَّذِي عَلَّمَ بِالْقَلَمِ عَلَّمَ الْإِنسَانَ مَا لَمْ يَعْلَمْ

Read! And your Lord is the Most Generous. Who has taught (the writing) by the pen.

He has taught man that which he knew not. (96:3-5)

AL-A'LAA

THE MOST HIGH

الأَعْلَى

سَبِّحِ اسْمَ رَبِّكَ الْأَعْلَى الَّذِي خَلَقَ فَسَوَّىٰ

Glorify the Name of your Lord, the Most High,

Who has created (everything), and then proportioned it. (87:1-2)

AL-'ALEEM

THE ALL-KNOWING

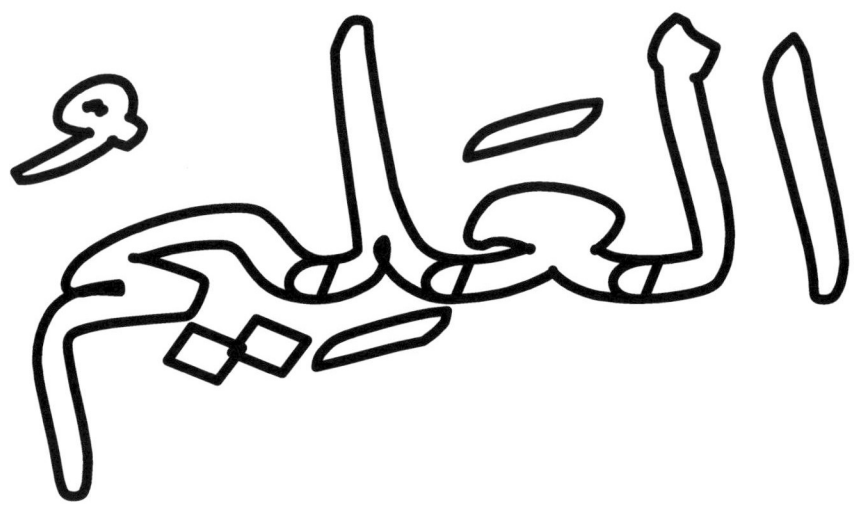

وَمَا تَدْرِي نَفْسٌ مَّاذَا تَكْسِبُ غَدًا ۖ وَمَا تَدْرِي نَفْسٌ بِأَيِّ أَرْضٍ تَمُوتُ ۚ إِنَّ اللَّهَ عَلِيمٌ خَبِيرٌ

No person knows what he will earn tomorrow, and no person knows in what land he will die.

Verily, Allah is All-Knowing, All-Aware. (31:34)

AL-'ALIYY

THE EXALTED

الْعَلِيُّ

لَهُ مَا فِي السَّمَاوَاتِ وَمَا فِي الْأَرْضِ ۖ وَهُوَ الْعَلِيُّ الْعَظِيمُ

To Him belongs all that is in the heavens and all that is in the earth,

and He is the Exalted, the Magnificent (42:4)

AL-AWWAL
THE FIRST

الأَوَّلُ

هُوَ الأَوَّلُ وَالآخِرُ وَالظَّاهِرُ وَالْبَاطِنُ ۖ وَهُوَ بِكُلِّ شَيْءٍ عَلِيمٌ

He is the First (nothing is before Him) and the Last (nothing is after Him), the Uppermost
(nothing is above Him) and the Innermost (nothing is nearer than Him). And He is the All-Knowing (57:3)

AL-'AZEEZ

THE MIGHTY

هُوَ الَّذِي يُصَوِّرُكُمْ فِي الْأَرْحَامِ كَيْفَ يَشَاءُ ۚ لَا إِلَٰهَ إِلَّا هُوَ الْعَزِيزُ الْحَكِيمُ

He it is Who shapes you in the wombs as He wills.

None has the right to be worshipped but He, the Mighty, the All-Wise. (3:6)

AL-BAARI'

THE ORIGINATOR, THE INVENTOR

هُوَ اللهُ الْخَالِقُ الْبَارِئُ

He is Allah, the Creator, the Inventor of all things (59:24)

AL-BAASIT

THE EXTENDER

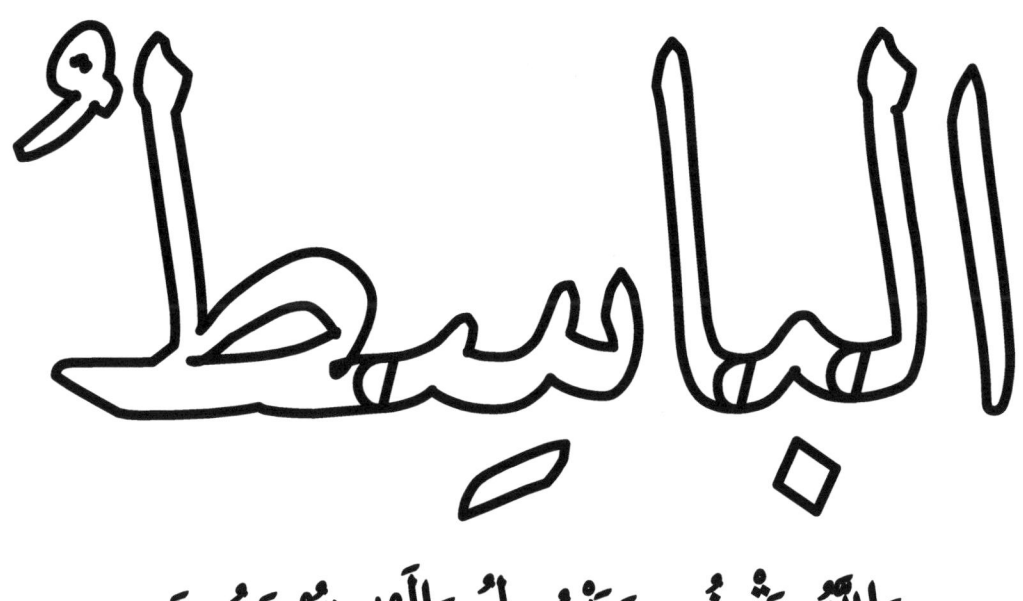

البَاسِطُ

وَاللّٰهُ يَقْبِضُ وَيَبْسُطُ وَإِلَيْهِ تُرْجَعُونَ

And it is Allah that withholds or extends (your provisions), and unto Him you shall return. (2:245)

AL-BAATIN
THE INNERMOST

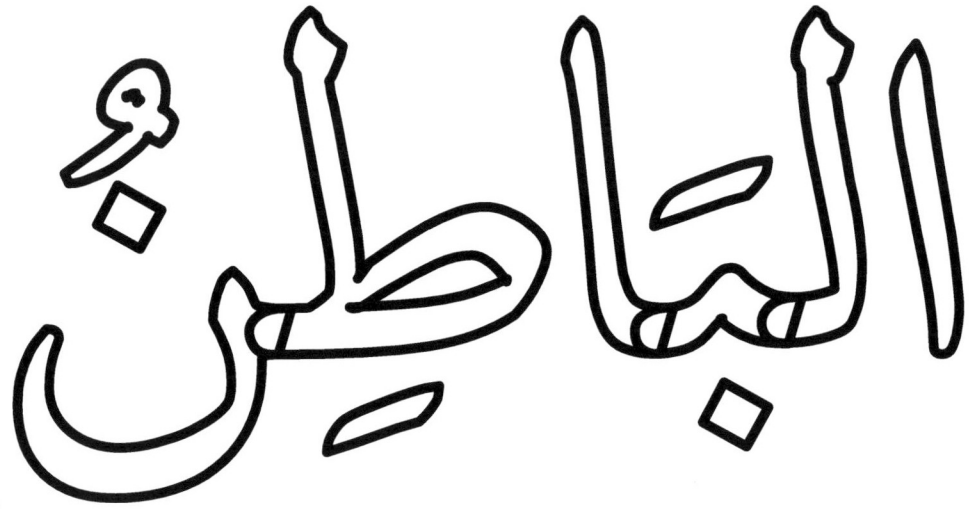

هُوَ الْأَوَّلُ وَالْآخِرُ وَالظَّاهِرُ وَالْبَاطِنُ ۖ وَهُوَ بِكُلِّ شَيْءٍ عَلِيمٌ

He is the First (nothing is before Him) and the Last (nothing is after Him), the Uppermost (nothing is above Him) and the Innermost (nothing is nearer than Him). And He is the All-Knowing (57:3)

AL-BARR

THE GENEROUS AND MOST COURTEOUS

إِنَّا كُنَّا مِن قَبْلُ نَدْعُوهُ ۖ إِنَّهُ هُوَ الْبَرُّ الرَّحِيمُ

"Verily, We used to invoke Him (Alone) before.

Verily, He is the Generous and Most Courteous, the Especially Merciful." (52:28)

AL-BASEER

THE ALL-SEEING

لَن تَنفَعَكُمْ أَرْحَامُكُمْ وَلَا أَوْلَادُكُمْ يَوْمَ الْقِيَامَةِ يَفْصِلُ بَيْنَكُمْ وَاللَّهُ بِمَا تَعْمَلُونَ بَصِيرٌ

Neither your relatives nor your children will benefit you on the Day of Resurrection.

He will judge between you. And Allah is All-Seeing of what you do. (60:3)

AL-FATTAH

THE JUDGE, THE OPENER

قُلْ يَجْمَعُ بَيْنَنَا رَبُّنَا ثُمَّ يَفْتَحُ بَيْنَنَا بِالْحَقِّ وَهُوَ الْفَتَّاحُ الْعَلِيمُ

Say: "Our Lord will assemble us all together (on the Day of Resurrection), then He will judge between us with truth. And He is the Judge, the All-Knowing (34:26)

AL-GHAFFAAR

THE EVER-FORGIVING

وَإِنِّي لَغَفَّارٌ لِّمَن تَابَ وَآمَنَ وَعَمِلَ صَالِحًا ثُمَّ اهْتَدَىٰ

And verily, I am indeed forgiving to him who repents, believes

and does righteous good deeds, and then remains constant in doing them. (20:82)

AL-GHAFOOR

THE GREAT FORGIVER

يَغْفِرُ لِمَن يَشَاءُ وَيُعَذِّبُ مَن يَشَاءُ ۚ وَاللَّهُ غَفُورٌ رَّحِيمٌ

He forgives whom He wills, and punishes whom He wills. And Allah is Forgiving, Merciful. (3:89)

AL-GHANIYY

THE RICH, THE SELF-SUFFICIENT

الغَنِيُّ

قَوْلٌ مَّعْرُوفٌ وَمَغْفِرَةٌ خَيْرٌ مِّن صَدَقَةٍ يَتْبَعُهَا أَذًى ۗ وَاللَّهُ غَنِيٌّ حَلِيمٌ

Kind words and forgiving of faults are better than Sadaqah (charity) followed by injury.

And Allah is Rich (Free of all needs) and Most-Forbearing. (2:263)

AL-HAAFIDH
THE PROTECTOR

قَالَ هَلْ آمَنُكُمْ عَلَيْهِ إِلَّا كَمَا أَمِنتُكُمْ عَلَىٰ أَخِيهِ مِن قَبْلُ ۖ فَاللَّهُ خَيْرٌ حَافِظًا

He said: "Can I entrust him to you except as I entrusted his brother

[Yusuf] to you aforetime? But Allah is the Protector (12:64)

AL-HAFEEDH
THE GUARDIAN

وَيَسْتَخْلِفُ رَبِّي قَوْمًا غَيْرَكُمْ وَلَا تَضُرُّونَهُ شَيْئًا ۚ إِنَّ رَبِّي عَلَىٰ كُلِّ شَيْءٍ حَفِيظٌ

My Lord will make another people succeed you, and you will not harm Him
in the least. Surely, my Lord is Guardian over all things." (11:57)

AL-HAFIYY

THE MOST GRACIOUS

قَالَ سَلَامٌ عَلَيْكَ ۖ سَأَسْتَغْفِرُ لَكَ رَبِّي ۖ إِنَّهُ كَانَ بِي حَفِيًّا

(Ibrahim) said: "Peace be on you! I will ask Forgiveness of my Lord

for you. Verily He is to me Most Gracious". (19:47)

AL-HAKAM

THE JUST JUDGE

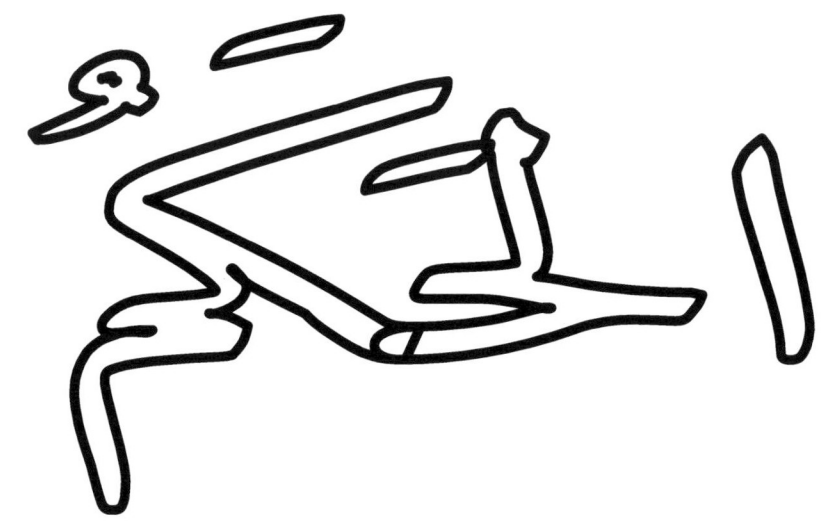

أَفَغَيْرَ اللَّهِ أَبْتَغِي حَكَمًا وَهُوَ الَّذِي أَنزَلَ إِلَيْكُمُ الْكِتَابَ مُفَصَّلًا

"Shall I seek a judge other than Allah while it is He Who has sent
down unto you the Book (the Qur'an), explained in detail." (6:114)

AL-HAKEEM

THE ALL-WISE

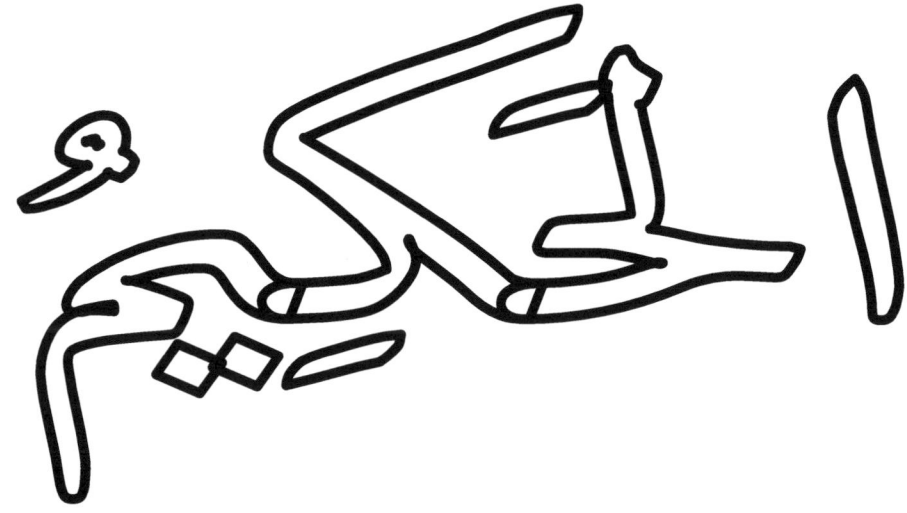

وَهُوَ الَّذِي فِي السَّمَاءِ إِلَهٌ وَفِي الْأَرْضِ إِلَهٌ ۚ وَهُوَ الْحَكِيمُ الْعَلِيمُ

It is He (Allah) Who is the only Ilah (God to be worshipped) in the heaven and the only Ilah

(God to be worshipped) on the earth. And He is the All-Wise, the All-Knowing. (43:84)

AL-HALEEM

THE FORBEARING

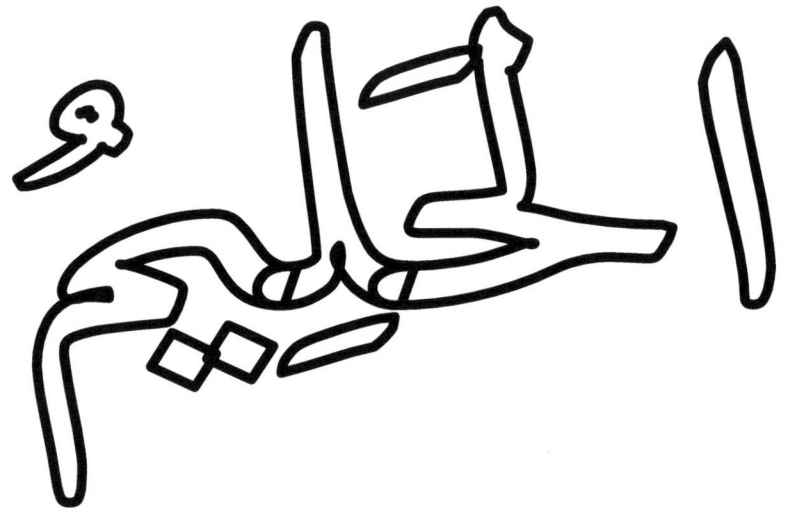

وَاعْلَمُوا أَنَّ اللَّهَ يَعْلَمُ مَا فِي أَنْفُسِكُمْ فَاحْذَرُوهُ ۚ وَاعْلَمُوا أَنَّ اللَّهَ غَفُورٌ حَلِيمٌ

And know that Allah knows what is in your minds, so fear Him.

And know that Allah is Oft-Forgiving, Most Forbearing. (2:235)

AL-HAMEED

THE PRAISEWORTHY

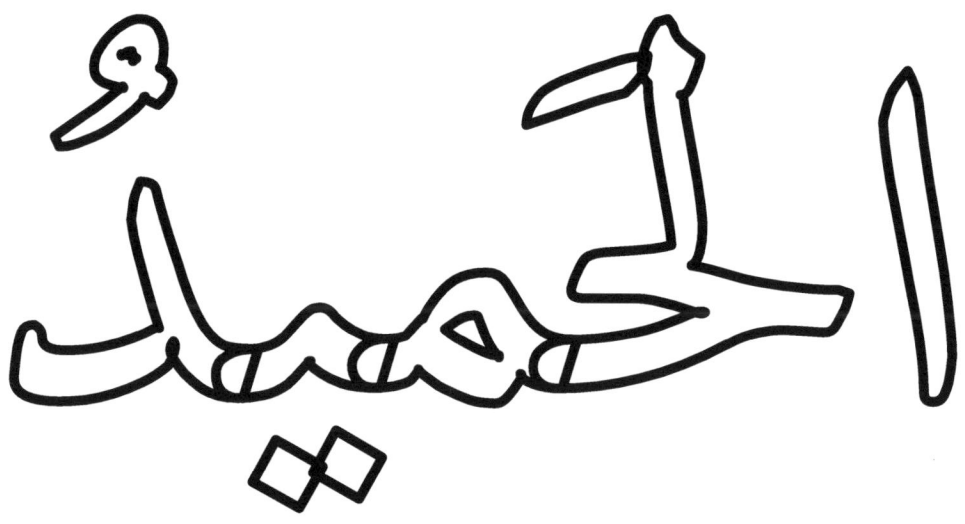

الر ۚ كِتَابٌ أَنزَلْنَاهُ إِلَيْكَ لِتُخْرِجَ النَّاسَ مِنَ الظُّلُمَاتِ إِلَى النُّورِ بِإِذْنِ رَبِّهِمْ إِلَى صِرَاطِ الْعَزِيزِ الْحَمِيدِ

Alif-Lam-Ra. A Book which We have revealed to you that you might bring mankind out

of darknesses into the light by permission of their Lord, to the path of the Almighty, the Praiseworthy (14:1)

AL-HAQQ

THE ULTIMATE TRUTH

وَقُلِ الْحَقُّ مِن رَّبِّكُمْ فَمَن شَاءَ فَلْيُؤْمِن وَمَن شَاءَ فَلْيَكْفُرْ

And say: "The Truth is from your Lord." Then whosoever wills,
let him believe; and whosoever wills, let him disbelieve. (18:29)

AL-HASEEB
THE RECKONER

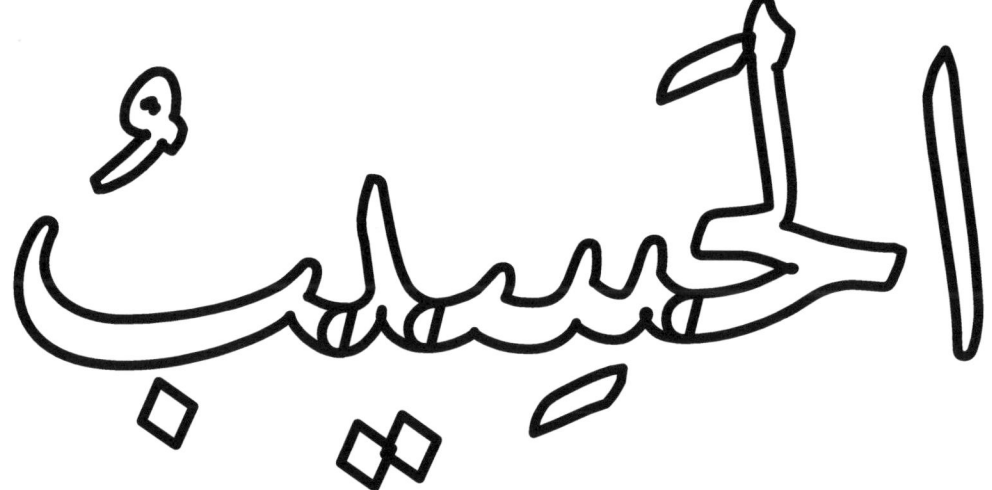

وَإِذَا حُيِّيتُم بِتَحِيَّةٍ فَحَيُّوا بِأَحْسَنَ مِنْهَا أَوْ رُدُّوهَا ۗ إِنَّ اللَّهَ كَانَ عَلَىٰ كُلِّ شَيْءٍ حَسِيبًا

When you are greeted with a greeting, greet in return with what is better than it,
or (at least) return it equally Certainly Allah is the Reckoner over all things (4:86)

AL-HAYY

THE EVER LIVING

اللَّهُ لَا إِلَهَ إِلَّا هُوَ الْحَيُّ الْقَيُّومُ

Allah - there is no deity worthy of worship except Him, the Ever-Living, the Sustainer of existence. (3:2)

AL-HAYYIYY

THE SHY AND MODEST ONE

إنَّ اللهَ حَيِيٌّ سِتِّيرٌ يُحِبُّ السِتْرَ

The Messenger of Allah صلى الله عليه وسلم said: "Allah is Shy and Modest and He loves Bashfulness and Modesty".

[Collected by Abu Dawood, An-Nissa'ee, Al-Baihaqee, Ahmed, and in Saheeh An-Nissa'ee.]

AL-ILAAH

THE ONLY ONE WHO DESERVES WORSHIP

وَهُوَ الَّذِي فِي السَّمَاءِ إِلَهٌ وَفِي الْأَرْضِ إِلَهٌ

It is He (Allah) Who is the only Ilah (God to be worshipped) in the
heaven and the only Ilah (God to be worshipped) on the earth. (43:84)

AL-JABBAAR

THE COMPELLOR AND RESTORER

هُوَ اللَّهُ الَّذِي لَا إِلَهَ إِلَّا هُوَ الْمَلِكُ الْقُدُّوسُ السَّلَامُ الْمُؤْمِنُ الْمُهَيْمِنُ الْعَزِيزُ الْجَبَّارُ

He is Allah beside Whom none has the right to be worshipped but He, the King, the Absolutely Pure, the One
Free from all imperfections, the Giver of security, the Watcher over His creatures, the Mighty, the Compellor ... (59:23)

AL-JAMEEL

THE BEAUTIFUL ONE

الجميل

إن الله جميل يحب الجمال

The Messenger of Allah ﷺ said: "Verily Allah is Beautiful and loves beauty".

[Sahih Muslim 1/164]

AL-JAWWAAD

THE MAGNANIMOUS

الْجَوَّادُ

إن الله تعالى جواد يحب الجود ، ويحب معالي الأخلاق ، ويكره سفسافها

"Allaah is Magnanimous and loves magnanimity, and He loves high morals, and He hates low morals."

[Classed as saheeh by al-Albaani in Saheeh al-Jaami' no. 1744.]

AL-KABEER

THE INCOMPARIBLY GREAT

عَالِمُ الْغَيْبِ وَالشَّهَادَةِ الْكَبِيرُ الْمُتَعَالِ

All-Knower of the Unseen and the seen, the Incomparably Great, the Supreme. (13:9)

AL-KAREEM
THE BOUNTIFUL, THE GENEROUS

يَا أَيُّهَا الْإِنسَانُ مَا غَرَّكَ بِرَبِّكَ الْكَرِيمِ

O man! What has made you careless about your Lord, the Generous? (82:6)

AL-KHAALIQ
THE CREATOR

لَا إِلَهَ إِلَّا هُوَ ۖ خَالِقُ كُلِّ شَيْءٍ فَاعْبُدُوهُ

None has the right to be worshipped but He, the Creator of all things, so worship Him (6:102)

AL-KHABEER

THE FULLY AWARE

وَمَا تَدْرِي نَفْسٌ مَّاذَا تَكْسِبُ غَدًا ۖ وَمَا تَدْرِي نَفْسٌ بِأَيِّ أَرْضٍ تَمُوتُ ۚ إِنَّ اللَّهَ عَلِيمٌ خَبِيرٌ

No person knows what he will earn tomorrow, and no person knows in what land he will die. Verily, Allah is All-Knowing, Fully Aware (31:34)

AL-KHALLAAQ

THE ONE WHO CREATES CONTINUOUSLY

إِنَّ رَبَّكَ هُوَ الْخَلَّاقُ الْعَلِيمُ

Verily, your Lord is the All-Knowing Continuous Creator. (15:86)

AL-LATEEF

THE MOST SUBTLE, THE KIND

أَلَمْ تَرَ أَنَّ اللَّهَ أَنزَلَ مِنَ السَّمَاءِ مَاءً فَتُصْبِحُ الْأَرْضُ مُخْضَرَّةً إِنَّ اللَّهَ لَطِيفٌ خَبِيرٌ

Do you not see that Allah sends down water (rain) from the sky, and then the
earth becomes green? Verily, Allah is the Most Kind, the Fully Aware (22:63)

AL-MAJEED

THE ONE PERFECT IN HONOUR AND GLORY

ذُو الْعَرْشِ الْمَجِيدُ

Owner of the Throne, the Glorious, (85:15)

AL-MALEEK

THE OMNIPOTENT SOVEREIGN

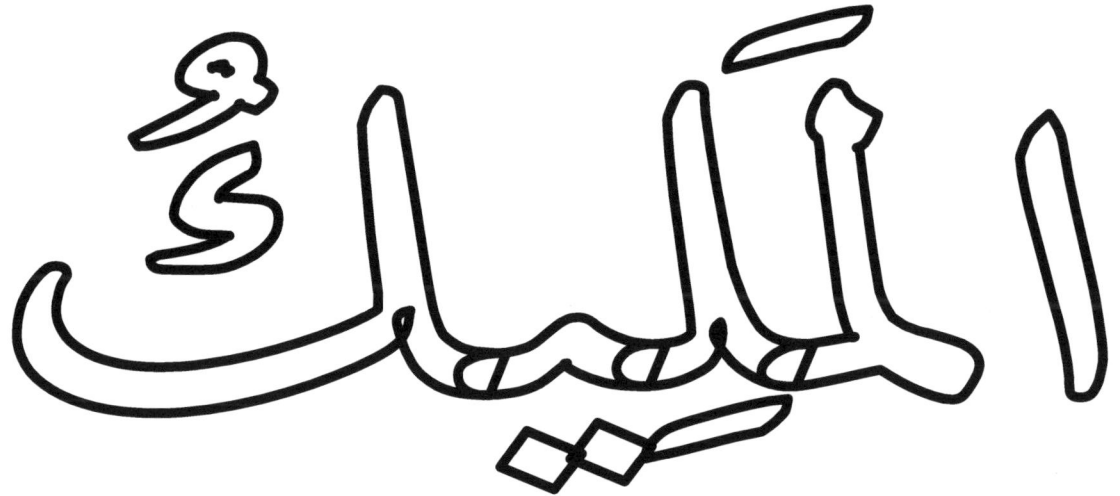

إِنَّ الْمُتَّقِينَ فِي جَنَّاتٍ وَنَهَرٍ فِي مَقْعَدِ صِدْقٍ عِندَ مَلِيكٍ مُّقْتَدِرٍ

Indeed, the righteous will be among gardens and rivers, in a seat of honour near an All-Powerful Sovereign. (54:54-55)

AL-MALIK

THE KING AND OWNER OF DOMINION

قُلِ اللَّهُمَّ مَالِكَ الْمُلْكِ تُؤْتِي الْمُلْكَ مَن تَشَاءُ وَتَنزِعُ الْمُلْكَ مِمَّن تَشَاءُ

Say: O Allah! Owner of the kingdom, You give the kingdom to whom
You will, and You take the kingdom from whom You will. (3:26)

AL-MANNAAN

THE BENEFICENT BESTOWER

اللهم إني أسألك بأن لك الحمد لا إله الا انت المنان بديع السموات والارض يا ذا الجلال والاكرام يا حى يا قيوم

"O Allah! I ask You because all praise is Yours. There is no true god except You, You are the One Who Bestows Favour, the Originator of the Heavens and Earth, Possessor of Majesty and Honour. O the Ever-Living, O Self-Subsisting.

[Du'aa recorded in Sunan Abu Dawood 8/1490]

AL-MATEEN
THE STRONG

إِنَّ اللَّهَ هُوَ الرَّزَّاقُ ذُو الْقُوَّةِ الْمَتِينُ

Verily, Allah is the Provider, Owner of Power, the Strong. (51:58)

AL-MAWLAA

THE LORD AND MASTER

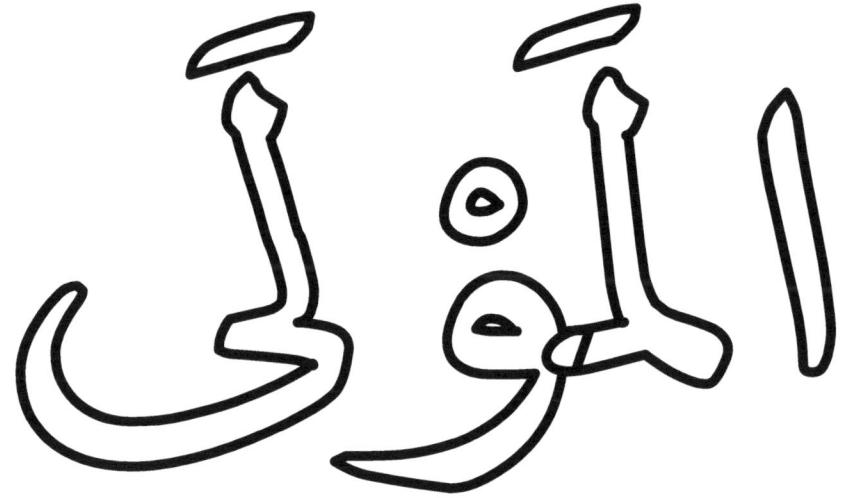

أَنتَ مَوْلَانَا فَانصُرْنَا عَلَى الْقَوْمِ الْكَافِرِينَ

You are our Mawlaa, so give us victory over the disbelieving people. (2:286)

AL-MU'AKHKHIR

THE ONE WHO DELAYS OR HOLDS BACK

أَنْتَ المُقَدِّمُ وَأَنْتَ المُؤَخِّرِ ، لا إِلهَ إِلاَّ أَنْت

"You are the One Who Brings Forth and You are the One Who Delays. There is none worthy of Worship but You."

[Du'aa (excerpt) recited after opening takbeer ~ Sahihain, Fathul Bari 3/3, 11/116, 13/371]

AL-MUBEEN

THE CLEAR AND MANIFEST

يَوْمَئِذٍ يُوَفِّيهِمُ اللَّهُ دِينَهُمُ الْحَقَّ وَيَعْلَمُونَ أَنَّ اللَّهَ هُوَ الْحَقُّ الْمُبِينُ

On that Day Allah will pay them the recompense of their deeds in full, and they will know that Allah, He is the Manifest Truth. (24:25)

AL-MUHAYMIN

THE PROTECTOR AND OVERSEER

هُوَ اللَّهُ الَّذِي لَا إِلَهَ إِلَّا هُوَ الْمَلِكُ الْقُدُّوسُ السَّلَامُ الْمُؤْمِنُ الْمُهَيْمِنُ

He is Allah beside Whom none has the right to be worshipped but He, the King, the Absolutely Pure,

the One Free from all imperfections, the Giver of security, the Watcher over His creatures. (59:23)

AL-MUHEET

THE ONE WHO FULLY COMPREHENDS

وَلَا تَكُونُوا كَالَّذِينَ خَرَجُوا مِن دِيَارِهِم بَطَرًا وَرِئَاءَ النَّاسِ وَيَصُدُّونَ عَن سَبِيلِ اللّٰهِ ۚ وَاللّٰهُ بِمَا يَعْمَلُونَ مُحِيطٌ

And be not like those who come out of their homes boastfully and to be seen of men, and hinder from the Path of Allah; and Allah Fully Comprehends all they do. (8:47)

AL-MUHSIN

THE ONE WHO DOES PERFECT GOOD

إِنَّ اللهَ تَعَالَى مُحْسِنٌ فَأَحْسِنُوا

The Messenger of Allah ﷺ said: "Allah, the Most High, is the One Who does Perfect Good, so do good."

[Reported by Ibn 'Adi on the authority of Sumurah ~ Sahih]

AL-MUJEEB
THE RESPONSIVE

فَاسْتَغْفِرُوهُ ثُمَّ تُوبُوا إِلَيْهِ ۚ إِنَّ رَبِّي قَرِيبٌ مُّجِيبٌ

Then ask forgiveness of Him and turn to Him in repentance.

Certainly, my Lord is Near (to all by His Knowledge), Responsive. (11:61)

AL-MU'MIN

THE ONE WHO GIVES EEMAAN AND SECURITY

هُوَ اللَّهُ الَّذِي لَا إِلَهَ إِلَّا هُوَ الْمَلِكُ الْقُدُّوسُ السَّلَامُ الْمُؤْمِنُ

He is Allah beside Whom none has the right to be worshipped but He, the King,

the Absolutely Pure, the One Free from all imperfections, the Giver of security ... (59:23)

AL-MUQADDIM

THE ONE WHO BRINGS FORWARD

أَنْتَ المُقَدِّمُ وَأَنْتَ المُؤَخِّرِ ، لا إِلهَ إِلاَّ أَنْت

"You are the One Who Brings Forth and You are the One Who Delays. There is none worthy of Worship but You."

[Du'aa (excerpt) recited after opening takbeer ~ Sahihain, Fathul Bari 3/3, 11/116, 13/371]

AL-MUQEET

THE ALL-ABLE MAINTAINER

مَّن يَشْفَعْ شَفَاعَةً حَسَنَةً يَكُن لَّهُ نَصِيبٌ مِّنْهَا ۖ وَمَن يَشْفَعْ شَفَاعَةً سَيِّئَةً يَكُن لَّهُ كِفْلٌ مِّنْهَا ۗ وَكَانَ اللهُ عَلَىٰ كُلِّ شَيْءٍ مُّقِيتًا

Whosoever intercedes for a good cause will have the reward thereof, and whosoever intercedes

for an evil cause will have a share in its burden. And Allah is Ever All-Able to do everything. (4:85)

AL-MUQTADIR

THE OMNIPOTENT

وَكَانَ اللّٰهُ عَلَىٰ كُلِّ شَيْءٍ مُّقْتَدِرًا

And Allah is ever, over all things, Omnipotent (18:45)

AL-MUSAWWIR
THE FASHIONER

هُوَ اللَّهُ الْخَالِقُ الْبَارِئُ الْمُصَوِّرُ

He is Allah, the Creator, the Inventor of all things, the Fashioner (59:24)

AL-MUTA'AALEE

THE SUPREME AND EXALTED

عَالِمُ الْغَيْبِ وَالشَّهَادَةِ الْكَبِيرُ الْمُتَعَالِ

All-Knower of the Unseen and the seen, the Incomparably Great, the Supreme. (13:9)

AL-MUTAKABBIR
THE SUPERIOR, THE MAJESTIC

هُوَ اللَّهُ الَّذِي لَا إِلَهَ إِلَّا هُوَ الْمَلِكُ الْقُدُّوسُ السَّلَامُ الْمُؤْمِنُ الْمُهَيْمِنُ الْعَزِيزُ الْجَبَّارُ الْمُتَكَبِّرُ

He is Allah beside Whom none has the right to be worshipped but He, the King, the Absolutely Pure, the One Free from all imperfections, the Giver of security, the Watcher over His creatures, the Mighty, the Compellor, the Superior (59:23)

AL-MU'TEE

THE GIVER

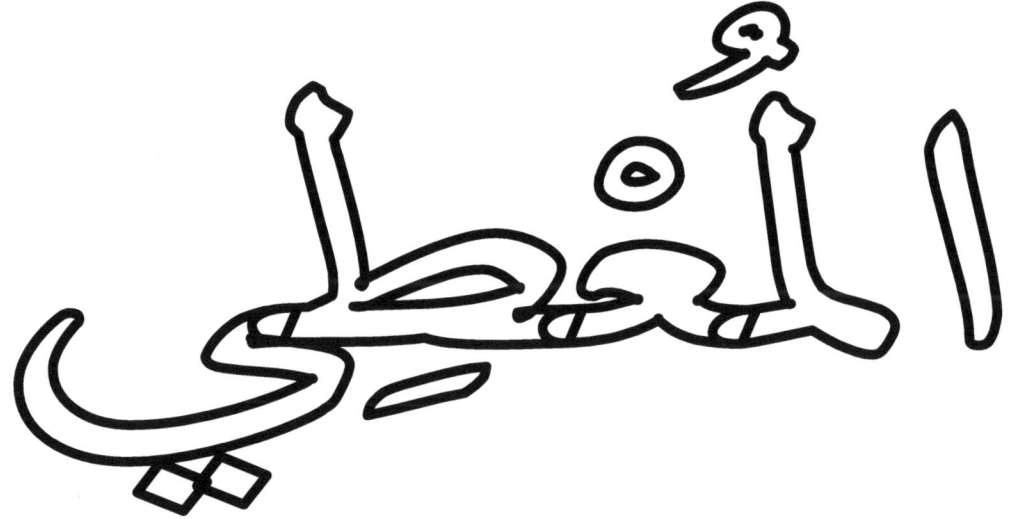

الله تعالى المعطي وأنا القاسم

The Messenger of Allah ﷺ said: "... Allah is the Giver and I am the distributor ..."

[Sahih Bukhari 53/346]

AL-QAABID

THE WITHHOLDER, THE RESTRICTOR

وَاللَّهُ يَقْبِضُ وَيَبْسُطُ وَإِلَيْهِ تُرْجَعُونَ

And it is Allah that withholds or extends (your provisions), and unto Him you shall return. (2:245)

AL-QAADIR

THE FULLY ABLE ONE

قُلْ هُوَ الْقَادِرُ عَلَى أَن يَبْعَثَ عَلَيْكُمْ عَذَابًا مِّن فَوْقِكُمْ أَوْ مِن تَحْتِ أَرْجُلِكُمْ

Say: "He is Fully Able to send punishment on you from above or from under your feet. (6:65)

AL-QAAHIR

THE INVINCIBLE SUBDUER

وَهُوَ الْقَاهِرُ فَوْقَ عِبَادِهِ ۚ وَهُوَ الْحَكِيمُ الْخَبِيرُ

And He is the Invincible Subduer above His slaves, and He is the All-Wise, the Fully Aware. (6:18)

AL-QADEER

THE ALL-POWERFUL, THE ABLE

أَيْنَ مَا تَكُونُوا يَأْتِ بِكُمُ اللَّهُ جَمِيعًا ۚ إِنَّ اللَّهَ عَلَىٰ كُلِّ شَيْءٍ قَدِيرٌ

Wheresoever you may be, Allah will bring you together (on the Day of Resurrection).

Truly, Allah is Able to do all things. (2:148)

AL-QAHHAAR

THE ALL-PREVAILING, THE SUBDUER

أَأَرْبَابٌ مُّتَفَرِّقُونَ خَيْرٌ أَمِ اللَّهُ الْوَاحِدُ الْقَهَّارُ

Are many different lords better or Allah, the One, the All-Prevailing? (12:39)

AL-QAREEB

THE ONE WHO IS NEAR

وَإِذَا سَأَلَكَ عِبَادِي عَنِّي فَإِنِّي قَرِيبٌ

And when My slaves ask you concerning Me, then (answer them),

I am indeed near (to them by My Knowledge). (2:186)

AL-QAWIYY

THE MIGHTY, THE OWNER OF POWER

الْقَوِيُّ

إِنَّ اللَّهَ هُوَ الرَّزَّاقُ ذُو الْقُوَّةِ الْمَتِينُ

Verily, Allah is the Provider, Owner of Power, the Strong. (51:58)

AL-QAYYOOM

THE SELF-SUSTAINING

الْقَيُّوم

وَعَنَتِ الْوُجُوهُ لِلْحَيِّ الْقَيُّومِ

And (all) faces shall be humbled before the Ever Living, the One Who sustains all that exists. (20:111)

AL-QUDDOOS

THE ABSOLUTELY PURE

يُسَبِّحُ لِلَّهِ مَا فِي السَّمَاوَاتِ وَمَا فِي الْأَرْضِ الْمَلِكِ الْقُدُّوسِ الْعَزِيزِ الْحَكِيمِ

Whatsoever is in the heavens and whatsoever is on the earth glorifies Allah,

the King (of everything), the Absolutely Pure, the All-Mighty, the All-Wise.(62:1)

AL-WAAHID

THE ONE, THE ONLY

الْوَاحِد

أَأَرْبَابٌ مُّتَفَرِّقُونَ خَيْرٌ أَمِ اللَّهُ الْوَاحِدُ الْقَهَّارُ

Are many different lords better or Allah, the One, the All-Prevailing? (12:39)

AL-WAARITH
THE INHERITOR

الْوَارِث

وَإِنَّا لَنَحْنُ نُحْيِي وَنُمِيتُ وَنَحْنُ الْوَارِثُونَ

And certainly We! We it is Who give life, and cause death, and We are the Inheritors. (15:23)

AL-WAASI'

THE ALL-ENCOMPASSING

وَاللَّهُ يُضَاعِفُ لِمَن يَشَاءُ وَاللَّهُ وَاسِعٌ عَلِيمٌ

Allah gives manifold increase to whom He wills. And Allah is All-Encompassing All-Knowing. (2:261)

AL-WADOOD
THE MOST LOVING

الْوَدُودُ

وَاسْتَغْفِرُوا رَبَّكُمْ ثُمَّ تُوبُوا إِلَيْهِ ۚ إِنَّ رَبِّي رَحِيمٌ وَدُودٌ

"And ask forgiveness of your Lord and turn unto Him in repentance. Verily, my Lord is Most Merciful, Most Loving." (11:90)

AL-WAHHAAB

THE GIVER OF GIFTS, THE BESTOWER

رَبَّنَا لَا تُزِغْ قُلُوبَنَا بَعْدَ إِذْ هَدَيْتَنَا وَهَبْ لَنَا مِن لَّدُنكَ رَحْمَةً ۚ إِنَّكَ أَنتَ الْوَهَّابُ

"Our Lord! Let not our hearts deviate after You have guided us, and grant us mercy from You. Truly, You are the Bestower." (3:8)

AL-WAKEEL

THE DISPOSER OF AFFAIRS

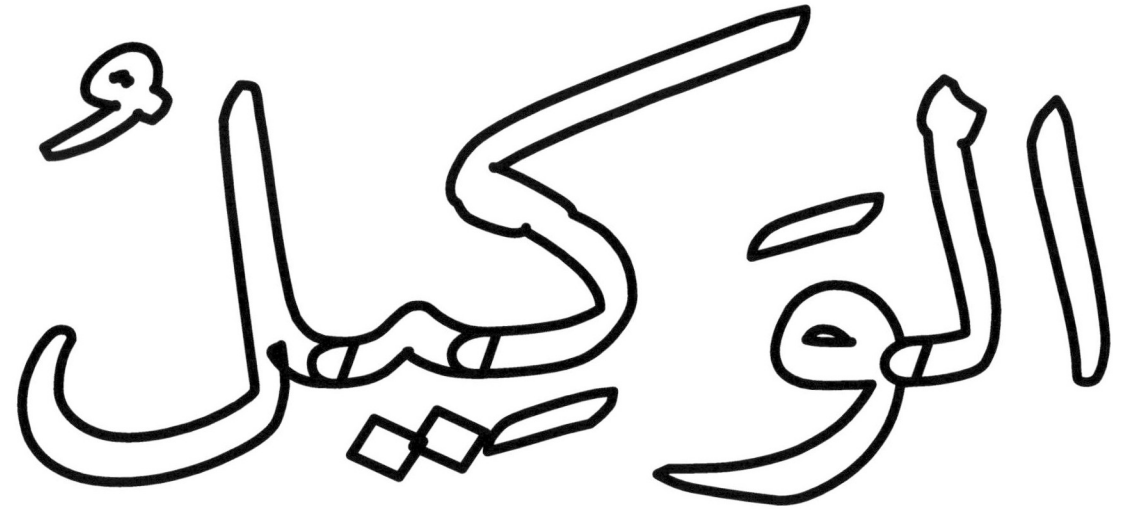

وَتَوَكَّلْ عَلَى اللهِ ۚ وَكَفَىٰ بِاللهِ وَكِيلًا

And put your trust in Allah, and Sufficient is Allah as a Wakeel (Disposer of affairs). (33:3)

AL-WALIYY

THE GUARDIAN LORD

أَمِ اتَّخَذُوا مِن دُونِهِ أَوْلِيَاءَ فَاللَّهُ هُوَ الْوَلِيُّ وَهُوَ يُحْيِي الْمَوْتَىٰ وَهُوَ عَلَىٰ كُلِّ شَيْءٍ قَدِيرٌ

Or have they taken (for worship) Auliya' besides Him? But Allah - He Alone is the Guardian Lord.

And it is He Who gives life to the dead, and He is Able to do all things. (42:9)

AL-WITR

THE ONE

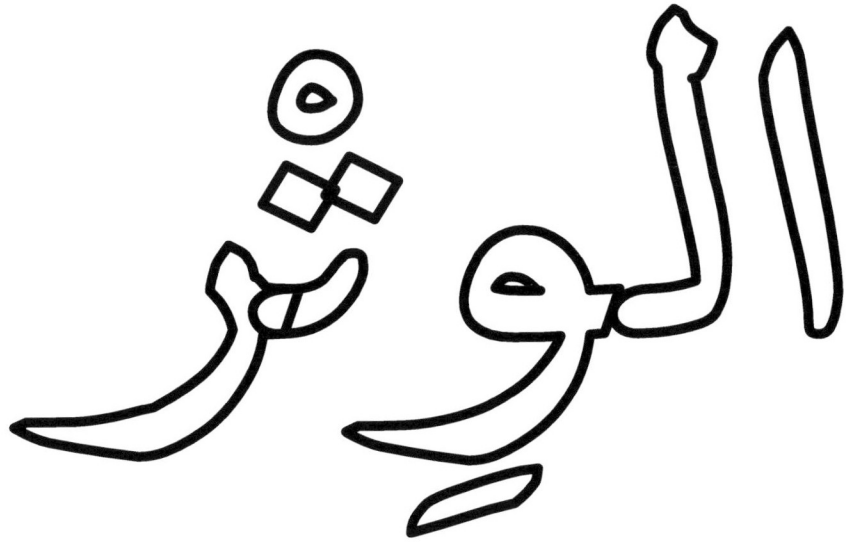

الْوِتْرُ

إن الله وتر يحب الوتر، فأوتروا يا أهل القرآن

The Messenger of Allah ﷺ said: "Allah is Witr (single, odd) and loves what is Witr. So perform Witr prayer.

O followers of Qur'an observe Witr (prayer)" [At-Tirmidhi and Abu Dawud]

AN-NASEER

THE HELPER

أَلَمْ تَعْلَمْ أَنَّ اللَّهَ لَهُ مُلْكُ السَّمَاوَاتِ وَالْأَرْضِ ۚ وَمَا لَكُم مِّن دُونِ اللَّهِ مِن وَلِيٍّ وَلَا نَصِيرٍ

Do you not know that it is Allah to Whom belongs the dominion of the heavens and the earth?

And besides Allah you have neither any Wali (protector or guardian) nor any helper. (2:107)

AR-RABB

THE LORD AND NURTURER

الرَّبّ

يَا أَيُّهَا النَّاسُ اعْبُدُوا رَبَّكُمُ الَّذِي خَلَقَكُمْ وَالَّذِينَ مِن قَبْلِكُمْ لَعَلَّكُمْ تَتَّقُونَ

O mankind! Worship your Lord, Who created you and those who were before you so that you may become Al-Muttaqun. (2:21)

AR-RAFEEQ

THE GENTLE

الرَّفِيقُ

قال ابن القيم وهو الرفيق يحب أهل الرفق بل يعطيهم بالرفق فوق أمان

Ibn al-Qayyim said: He is Gentle and loves people who are gentle;

by His gentleness He gives them more than they can wish for.

AR-RAHEEM

THE ESPECIALLY MERCIFUL

إِنَّهُ هُوَ التَّوَّابُ الرَّحِيمُ

Truly, He is the One Who accepts repentance, the Especially Merciful. (2:54)

AR-RAHMAN

THE ENTIRELY MERCIFUL

قُلِ ادْعُوا اللَّهَ أَوِ ادْعُوا الرَّحْمَٰنَ ۖ أَيًّا مَّا تَدْعُوا فَلَهُ الْأَسْمَاءُ الْحُسْنَىٰ

Say: Invoke Allah or invoke the Entirely Merciful, by whatever name
you invoke Him (it is the same), for to Him belong the Best Names. (17:110)

AR-RA'OOF

THE COMPASSIONATE AND KIND

وَمَا كَانَ اللّٰهُ لِيُضِيعَ إِيمَانَكُمْ ۚ إِنَّ اللّٰهَ بِالنَّاسِ لَرَءُوفٌ رَّحِيمٌ

And Allah would never make your faith (prayers) to be lost.

Truly, Allah is full of Kindness, Especially Merciful. (2:143)

AR-RA'OOF

THE COMPASSIONATE AND KIND

الرَّؤُوفُ

وَمَا كَانَ اللّٰهُ لِيُضِيعَ إِيمَانَكُمْ ۚ إِنَّ اللّٰهَ بِالنَّاسِ لَرَءُوفٌ رَّحِيمٌ

And Allah would never make your faith (prayers) to be lost.

Truly, Allah is full of Kindness, Especially Merciful. (2:143)

AR-RAQEEB

THE ALL-WATCHFUL

وَاتَّقُوا اللَّهَ الَّذِي تَسَاءَلُونَ بِهِ وَالْأَرْحَامَ ۚ إِنَّ اللَّهَ كَانَ عَلَيْكُمْ رَقِيبًا

And fear Allah through Whom you demand (your mutual rights), and (do not cut the relations of) the wombs (kinship) . Surely, Allah is All-Watchful over you. (4:1)

AR-RAZZAAQ

THE PROVIDER

مَا أُرِيدُ مِنْهُم مِّن رِّزْقٍ وَمَا أُرِيدُ أَن يُطْعِمُونِ إِنَّ اللَّهَ هُوَ الرَّزَّاقُ

I seek not any provision from them nor do I ask that they should feed Me.

Verily, Allah is the Provider (51:57-58)

ASH-SHAAFEE
THE HEALER

المُشَافِي

وَإِذَا مَرِضْتُ فَهُوَ يَشْفِينِ

"And when I am ill, it is He who cures me. (26:80)

ASH-SHAAKIR

THE RECOGNISER AND REWARDER OF GOOD

وَمَن تَطَوَّعَ خَيْرًا فَإِنَّ اللَّهَ شَاكِرٌ عَلِيمٌ

And whoever does good voluntarily, then verily, Allah is the Recogniser of Good, All-Knowing. (2:158)

ASH-SHAHEED

THE WITNESS

هُوَ الَّذِي أَرْسَلَ رَسُولَهُ بِالْهُدَىٰ وَدِينِ الْحَقِّ لِيُظْهِرَهُ عَلَى الدِّينِ كُلِّهِ ۚ وَكَفَىٰ بِاللَّهِ شَهِيدًا

He it is Who has sent His Messenger with guidance and the Religion of Truth (Islam),
that He may make it superior to all religions. And sufficient is Allah as a Witness (48:28)

ASH-SHAKOOR
THE APPRECIATIVE

المُشَكُورُ

إِن تُقْرِضُوا اللَّهَ قَرْضًا حَسَنًا يُضَاعِفْهُ لَكُمْ وَيَغْفِرْ لَكُمْ وَاللَّهُ شَكُورٌ حَلِيمٌ

If you lend Allah a goodly loan, He will double it for you, and will forgive you.

And Allah is Most Appreciative, Most Forbearing, (64:17)

AS-SALAAM

THE PERFECTION AND GIVER OF PEACE

هُوَ اللَّهُ الَّذِي لَا إِلَهَ إِلَّا هُوَ الْمَلِكُ الْقُدُّوسُ السَّلَامُ

He is Allah beside Whom none has the right to be worshipped but He,

the King, the Absolutely Pure, the One Free from all imperfections ... (59:23)

AS-SAMAD

THE SELF-SUFFICIENT MASTER

قُلْ هُوَ اللَّهُ أَحَدٌ اللَّهُ الصَّمَدُ

Say: "He is Allah, (the) One (who is Unique). Allah, the Self-Sufficient Master (112:1-2)

AS-SAMEE'

THE ALL-HEARING

المَسْمِيعُ

وَاللَّهُ يَقْضِي بِالْحَقِّ ۖ وَالَّذِينَ يَدْعُونَ مِن دُونِهِ لَا يَقْضُونَ بِشَيْءٍ ۗ إِنَّ اللَّهَ هُوَ السَّمِيعُ البَصِيرُ

And Allah judges with truth, while those to whom they invoke besides Him, cannot judge anything.

Certainly, Allah! He is the All-Hearing, the All-Seeing. (40:20)

AS-SAYYID

THE MASTER

السَّيِّدُ اللهُ تَبَارَكَ وَتَعَالَى

The Messenger of Allah ﷺ said: "The Master is Allah, the Blessed and Most High".

[Sunan Abu Dawud 41/4788]

AS-SUBOOH
THE GLORIFIED, THE PERFECT

السَّبُّوحُ

سُبُّوحٌ قُدُّوسٌ، رَبُّ الملائِكَةِ وَالرُّوحِ

"Glorified, Most Holy, Lord of the Angels and the Spirit".

[Du'aa to recite in Sujood ~ Sahih Muslim 1/353, Abu Dawood 1/230]

AT-TAWWAB

THE ONE WHO ACCEPTS REPENTANCE

أَلَمْ يَعْلَمُوا أَنَّ اللَّهَ هُوَ يَقْبَلُ التَّوْبَةَ عَنْ عِبَادِهِ وَيَأْخُذُ الصَّدَقَاتِ وَأَنَّ اللَّهَ هُوَ التَّوَّابُ الرَّحِيمُ

Do they not know that it is Allah who accepts repentance from His slaves and acknowledges their charity, and that it is Allah who is the Accepting of repentance, the Especially Merciful? (9:104)

AT-TAYYIB
THE PURE ONE

الطّيّبُ

إن الله تعالى طيب لا يقبل إلا طيبا

The Messenger of Allah ﷺ said: "Verily, Allah, the Most High, is Pure and only accepts that which is pure".

[Narrated by Abu Hurayrah ~ Sahih Muslim]

18196650R00059

Printed in Poland
by Amazon Fulfillment
Poland Sp. z o.o., Wrocław